Alexander Hamilton

Heroes of the American Revolution

Don McLeese

Rourke
Publishing LLC
Vero Beach, Florida 32964

www.rourkepublishing.com

PHOTO CREDITS: Cover Scene, Title page, Pages 4, 5, 13, 14, 17, 19, 20, 24, 29
©North Wind Picture Archives; Cover Portrait, Pages 6, 9, 23, 27 from the
Library of Congress; Page 10 ©Artville

Title page: *The first meeting of Alexander Hamilton (right) and
George Washington (left)*

Editor: Frank Sloan

Cover and page design by Nicola Stratford

Library of Congress Cataloging-in-Publication Data

McLeese, Don.
  Alexander Hamilton / Don McLeese.
      p. cm. -- (Heroes of the American Revolution)
  Includes bibliographical references and index.
  ISBN 1-59515-219-9 (hardcover)
  1. Hamilton, Alexander, 1757-1804--Juvenile literature. 2. Statesmen--United
States--Biography--Juvenile literature. 3. United States--History--Revolution,
1775-1783--Juvenile literature. 4. United States--Politics and government--1783-
1809--Juvenile literature. I. Title.
E302.6.H2M43 2004
973.4'092--dc22

                              2004007603

Printed in the USA
LB/LB

Table of Contents

★

Alexander Hamilton was a great leader during the early years of the United States of America. He was known as a very smart man with a lot of great ideas. He called himself a "federalist," because he believed the country should have a strong **federal** (or central) government. He was the leader of the Federalist Party, one of the first political parties in the new country. He also helped write a book titled *The Federalist*.

Not everyone agreed with Hamilton's belief that the federal government should be strong. Thomas Jefferson argued with Hamilton that the states should have more power to make their own laws and that the federal government shouldn't have as much power.

The title page of The Federalist

A portrait of Alexander Hamilton

On horseback, George Washington takes command of the American army.

Alexander Hamilton was a close assistant to General George Washington, head of the army during the Revolutionary War. When Washington was elected to be the country's first president, Hamilton became the first secretary of the **treasury**, a powerful position in charge of money. If you look on a ten-dollar bill, you'll see a picture of Alexander Hamilton on the front of it.

Though Hamilton never became president, he showed people that the new country should have a balance between the powers of the federal government and the powers of the state government. To this day, American political figures continue to debate which should be stronger.

Born on an Island

★

Alexander Hamilton was born on January 11, 1755. (For some reason, he said he was born in 1757, but **historians** now believe the earlier date was true.) He lived on an island called Nevis in the West Indies, not far from America. During that era, America was ruled by England and so were these islands.

Hamilton's family didn't have much money. His parents weren't even married. His father, James Hamilton, had come from Scotland. His mother, Rachel Faucitt Lavien, had some family in France. Alexander had a brother, James, who was two years older.

An island in the West Indies that may be Nevis

This map shows the island of Nevis, where Hamilton was born.

Bahamas

Atlantic Ocean

Nevis

Caribbean Sea

Early Years

★

When Alexander was only 11, his father left the family. Before leaving in 1766, James had moved his family to another island named St. Croix, which is one of the Virgin Islands. Rachel opened a store to try to make money to feed her children after their father left. She also taught her children at home, since they had no money for school. Alexander learned to read French as well as English from his mother.

Later, a minister gave the family money for schooling. Alexander showed that he was very smart, with a good head for numbers as well as for reading.

THE CARIBBEAN SEA

This sea is south of what is now Florida and has the Virgin Islands, the West Indies, and many other islands in it.

~

On Their Own

★

In 1768, when Alexander was only 13 years old, his mother died, leaving her two sons all alone. James went to work with a carpenter, learning that trade. Alexander went to work for a company that sent **products** from St. Croix to other countries and brought products to the island.

TRADING COMPANIES

The company where Alexander worked was called a trading company. St. Croix had a lot of sugar, so the company sent sugar from St. Croix for a variety of different foods and products from other countries.

~

Alexander's boss, Nicholas Cruger, was from a rich family in New York. Nicholas knew that Alexander was a good worker and very smart, but that he had little money. The company where Alexander worked raised money to send him to school in New York.

Natives harvest sugarcane.

A formal portrait showing Alexander Hamilton seated at his desk

Becoming an American

In 1773, Alexander came to New York. He had letters with him from his boss, telling important people in New York that they should help Alexander. He continued his education by attending high school and college with the money that had been raised for him. He proved to be a very good student.

Hamilton became a writer, and some of his papers on politics were widely read, even while he was still a teenager. He wrote that America should become its own country, rather than being ruled by England. He signed these papers or pamphlets "A Friend of America," instead of using his real name. Readers were later surprised to learn that this "friend" was only a college student. He wrote so well and made such strong arguments that these pamphlets seemed like the work of an older, more powerful **political** leader.

★

Alexander Hamilton was only 21 years old when the Revolutionary War began in 1776. He was still in college, but he quit in order to help America win its **freedom** from England. He was a captain in the army in 1776-77 and then joined the staff of General George Washington, who was head of the American army. Hamilton became one of Washington's most trusted helpers and best friends.

GEORGE WASHINGTON

After the army that he led won the war for **independence** from England, Washington became the first president of the United States.

~

Hamilton fought in the Revolutionary War as an artillery officer.

Husband and Father

★

In 1780, Hamilton married Elizabeth Schuyler from New York. Not only did he love her, but her family also had a lot of money and was powerful in politics. Since Hamilton had come from a poor family, this was a big change for him. He and Elizabeth raised a big family of eight children. Alexander Hamilton continued his studies and became a lawyer. He also became involved with the new government of the United States of America. He was elected to Congress and was chosen to go to the **convention** that would write the Constitution, the rules for governing this new country.

THE CONSTITUTIONAL CONVENTION

The convention to write a **constitution** for the United States was held in Philadelphia in May, 1787.

~

Concerned people met for the Constitutional Convention in 1787.

Floats are shown in a parade that honored Hamilton after the Constitution was signed.

The New Country

Once America won the war with England, there was a new country: the United States of America. This new country needed its own rules. Alexander Hamilton believed strongly in the Constitution and helped get it approved. The Constitution showed which powers belonged to the federal government and which ones belonged to the states.

The Federalist

★

Alexander Hamilton believed that the federal government should be stronger than the states. Two other political leaders named John Jay and James Madison thought the same way that Alexander did. In 1777-78, all three of them wrote letters to newspapers about the need for a strong federal government. These letters were collected and published in a famous book titled *The Federalist*.

JOHN JAY AND JAMES MADISON

John Jay became the first Chief Justice of the U.S. Supreme Court. James Madison became the fourth U.S. president.

~

A portrait of James Madison

Hamilton, Washington, and other members of the president's cabinet

Secretary of the Treasury

★

When George Washington was elected the country's first president in 1789, he made Alexander Hamilton his first secretary of the treasury. This was a powerful position, and Hamilton helped to decide how the new country should deal with money, set up banks, and pay back other countries that had given America support in the war with England.

The secretaries of the various departments appointed by President Washington have become known as the **Cabinet**. Another member of Washington's cabinet was Thomas Jefferson, the secretary of state. Hamilton and Jefferson disagreed about government. Unlike Hamilton, Jefferson believed that each state government should have more power than the federal government.

THE CABINET

Even today the close advisers to the president who are head of important departments are known as the cabinet. Each adviser is called a "secretary" (secretary of defense, secretary of state, and so on).

~

Party Leaders

★

Because of their differences, these two became leaders in the forming of two political parties. Hamilton's was called the Federalist Party. Jefferson's was called the Democratic-Republican Party. There is no longer a Federalist Party, though Hamilton's ideas about government are still considered very important.

THE FEDERALIST PARTY

The Federalist Party was one of the first two political parties in the United States. The other was known as the Democratic-Republican. Today, the two leading parties are the Democratic and the Republican.

~

A portrait of Thomas Jefferson

Deciding the Presidency

★

Alexander Hamilton quit being secretary of the treasury in 1795. In 1800, the election for president between Thomas Jefferson and Aaron Burr ended in a tie. Alexander decided to support Jefferson, and he won. Burr never forgave Alexander. In 1804, Burr wanted to run for governor of New York, and he blamed Alexander when he did not get his party's nomination. Because of this, Burr challenged Hamilton to a duel. On July 11, 1804, the two men fought their duel, and Burr shot Hamilton, who died.

Though he never became president, Alexander Hamilton is remembered as one of the greatest political thinkers and most powerful leaders of the Revolutionary War era. He helped convince America that it should become its own country. He fought for its freedom and helped the government of the new country that resulted: the United States of America.

Hamilton was killed in a duel with Aaron Burr.

Time Line

1755	H	Alexander Hamilton is born.
1768	H	Alexander's mother dies.
1773	H	Alexander comes to New York.
1776	H	The Revolutionary War begins.
1776~77	H	Hamilton is a captain in the army.
1777~78	H	Hamilton, John Jay, and James Madison write letters to newspapers, later published in *The Federalist*.
1780	H	Hamilton marries Elizabeth Schuyler.
1787	H	Constitutional Convention is held in May.
1789	H	George Washington is elected president of the United States.
1800	H	Thomas Jefferson wins the election against Aaron Burr.
1804	H	Burr wants to be governor of New York but does not get his party's nomination.
1804	H	Burr challenges Hamilton to a duel and kills him.

Glossary

cabinet (KAB uh nut) — a group of close advisers to the
president who are heads of important government departments

constitution (KON stuh TOO shun) — the basic principles of a
country or state and the most important government document

convention (kon VEN shun) — a meeting where representatives
of different states decide and vote upon something

federal (FED uh rul) — a form of government in which power is
shared between the national (or federal) government and
the states

freedom (FREE dum) — the state of being free

historians (his TOR ee anz) — people who are experts in the
study of history

independence (IN duh PEN dunts) — freedom from another
government

political (po LIT ih kul) — relating to government and elections

products (PRAHD uctz) — things grown or made to be sold

treasury (TREZH uh ree) — the department of the government
in charge of money and finance

Index

Further Reading

Collier, James Lincoln. *The Alexander Hamilton You Never Knew* (You Never Knew Series). Scholastic Library Publishing, 2003

Decarolis, Lisa. *Alexander Hamilton: Federalist and Founding Father.* The Rosen Publishing Group, 2003

Degraw, Aleine. *Alexander Hamilton: American Statesman.* The Rosen Publishing Group, 2003

Websites to Visit

http://www.infoplease.com/ce6/people/A0822513.html
http://www.isidore-of-seville.com/hamilton/

About the Author

Don McLeese is an award-winning journalist whose work has appeared in many newspapers and magazines. He earned his M.A. degree in English from the University of Chicago, taught feature writing at the University of Texas and has frequently contributed to the World Book Encyclopedia. He lives with his wife and two daughters in West Des Moines, Iowa.